Thanksgiving

Jokes

Johnny B. Laughing

Johnny B. Laughing, The Joke King

Published by Johnny B. Laughing Joke Books.

Created in the U.S.A.

ISBN: 9781973211013

DEDICATION

THIS BOOK IS DEDICATED TO YOU, THE READER. IT'S A REAL PLEASURE CREATING THESE SILLY JOKE BOOKS FOR YOU TO ENJOY. SHARE THE GIFT OF LAUGHTER WITH A FRIEND!

TABLE OF CONTENTS

THANKSGIVING JOKES

Q: WHY DID THE TURKEY JOIN A BAND?

A: HE HAD THE DRUMSTICKS!

Q: WHAT WAS THE TURKEY'S RING TONE?

A: WING! WING!

Q: WHO IS NEVER HUNGRY AT THANKSGIVING?

A: THE TURKEY BECAUSE HE IS ALWAYS STUFFED!

Q: CAN YOU SPELL INDIAN HOUSE WITH TWO LETTERS?

A: TP!

Q: WHY WAS THE TURKEY ARRESTED?

A: HE WAS CONVICTED OF FOWL PLAY!

Q: IF APRIL SHOWERS BRING MAY FLOWERS, WHAT BROUGHT THE PILGRIMS?

A: SHIPS!

Q: WHERE DID THE PILGRIMS LAND WHEN THEY CAME TO AMERICA?

A: ON THEIR FEET!

Q: WHAT DO VAMPIRES PUT ON THEIR TURKEY?

A: GRAVE-Y!

Q: WHAT DID THE BABY CORN SAY TO MAMA CORN?

A: WHERE IS POP CORN?

Q: WHAT KIND OF KEY CANNOT UNLOCK A DOOR?

A: A TURKEY!

Q: WHAT BIRD HAS WINGS BUT CANNOT FLY?

A: A ROASTED TURKEY!

Q: IF THE PILGRIMS AND INDIANS WERE STILL ALIVE TODAY, WHAT WOULD THEY BE MOST FAMOUS FOR?

A: THEIR AGE!

Q: WHAT ALWAYS COMES AT THE BEGINNING OF A PARADE?

A: THE LETTER P!

Q: WHAT PART OF THE TURKEY HAS THE MOST FEATHERS?

A: THE OUTSIDE!

Q: WHAT DO SNOWMEN EAT FOR THANKSGIVING?

A: ICE-BURGERS!

Q: WHY DID THE TURKEY LAY AN EGG?

A: BECAUSE IF SHE DROPPED IT, IT WOULD BREAK!

Q: WHAT DO YOU GET WHEN YOU CROSS A TURKEY AND A BANJO?

A: A TURKEY THAT WILL PLUCK ITSELF!

Q: WHAT DID THE MONSTER SAY TO THE THANKSGIVING TURKEY?

A: PLEASED TO EAT YOU!

Q: WHAT IS PURPLE AND HAS LOTS OF FEATHERS?

A: A TURKEY HOLDING ITS BREATH!

Q: DID YOU HEAR ABOUT THE CONFUSED TURKEY?

A: HE WAS LOOKING FORWARD TO THANKSGIVING!

Q: WHAT DO YOU GET WHEN YOU CROSS A MONSTER WITH A THANKSGIVING DESSERT?

A: BUMPKIN PIE!

Q: WHAT DO YOU GET WHEN A TURKEY LAYS AN EGG ON TOP OF A HOUSE?

A: AN EGGROLL!

Q: WHY DID THE TURKEY CROSS THE ROAD?

A: TO PROVE TO EVERYONE THAT HE WAS NOT A CHICKEN!

Q: WHAT SHOULD YOU WEAR TO A THANKSGIVING EVENT?

A: A HAR-VEST!

Q: WHY DID A TURKEY SIT ON THE TOMAHAWK?

A: TO HATCHET!

Q: WHAT IS A PUMPKIN'S FAVORITE GAME?

A: SQUASH!

Q: HOW DOES THANKSGIVING ALWAYS END?

A: WITH A G!

Q: WHAT IS BROWN AND WHITE AND FLYING ALL OVER?

A: A THANKSGIVING TURKEY BEING SLICED BY A CHAIN SAW!

Q: WHAT DO VAMPIRES CALL THANKSGIVING?

A: FANGS-GIVING

Q: WHAT DID THE TURKEY SAY TO THE TURKEY HUNTER?

A: QUACK! QUACK!

Q: WHY DID THE PILGRIM'S PANTS KEEP FALLING OFF?

A: BECAUSE THEY WORE THEIR BELT BUCKLES ON THEIR HATS!

Q: WHICH COUNTRY DOES NOT CELEBRATE THANKSGIVING?

A: TURKEY!

Q: WHAT HAPPENED TO THE PILGRIM THAT STAYED IN THE SUN TOO LONG?

A: HE GOT A PURI-TAN!

Q: WHY WAS THANKSGIVING CREATED?

A: IT WAS ANOTHER EXCUSE TO WATCH FOOTBALL!

Q: WHAT IS THE MOST MUSICAL THING ABOUT A TURKEY?

A: DRUMSTICKS!

Q: WHY DID THE MONSTER GET FINED ON THANKSGIVING?

A: HE HAD EXCEEDED THE FEED LIMIT!

Q: WHY DID THE CRANBERRIES TURN RED?

A: THEY SAW THE TURKEY DRESSING!

Q: WHAT SMELLS REALLY GOOD AT THANKSGIVING?

A: YOUR NOSE!

Q: HOW DO YOU KNOW THE INDIANS WERE THE FIRST PEOPLE IN NORTH AMERICA?

A: THEY HAD RESERVATIONS!

Q: WHAT DO YOU GET WHEN YOU CROSS A MONSTER AND A TURKEY?

A: THE POULTRYGEIST!

Q: WHY WAS THE THANKSGIVING SOUP WORTH SO MUCH?

A: IT WAS MADE WITH 24 CARROTS!

Q: WHAT WAS THE TURKEY'S FAVORITE DESSERT?

A: BLUEBERRY COBBLER!

Q: WHAT HAPPENED TO THE PILGRIM THAT WAS SHOT AT?

A: HE HAD AN ARROW ESCAPE!

Q: WHY DID THE PILGRIMS WANT TO COME TO AMERICA IN THE SPRING?

A: APRIL SHOWERS BRING MAYFLOWERS!

Q: WHAT DID THE GENERAL DO ON THANKSGIVING?

A: HE GAVE TANKS!

Q: WHAT IS THE BEST THING TO PUT INTO A PUMPKIN PIE?

A: YOUR TEETH!

Q: WHAT NOISE DOES A SPACE TURKEY MAKE?

A: HUBBLE HUBBLE!

Q: WHAT IS A PILGRIM'S FAVORITE DANCE?

A: THE PLYMOUTH ROCK!

Q: WHY CAN'T YOU TAKE A TURKEY TO CHURCH?

A: THEY USE FOWL LANGUAGE!

Q: WHY DID THE PILGRIMS EAT TURKEY ON THANKSGIVING?

A: THEY COULD NOT FIT A COW IN THE OVEN!

Q: HOW DO YOU STUFF A TURKEY?

A: TAKE HIM TO AN ALL-YOU-CAN-EAT-BUFFET!

Q: WHAT DO YOU GET WHEN YOU CROSS A TURKEY AND AN OCTOPUS?

A: ENOUGH DRUMSTICKS TO FEED THE ENTIRE SCHOOL!

Q: WHAT HAPPENED WHEN THE TURKEY GOT INTO A FIGHT?

A: HE GOT THE STUFFING BEAT OUT OF HIM!

Q: WHAT IS THE DIFFERENCE BETWEEN HALLOWEEN AND THANKSGIVING?

A: ONE HAS GOBLINS AND THE OTHER HAS GOBBLERS!

Q: WHAT DID THE MATH TEACHER BRING TO THE THANKSGIVING FEAST?

A: PUMPKIN PI!

KNOCK KNOCK!

WHO'S THERE?

GLADYS!

GLADYS WHO?

AREN'T YOU GLADYS
THANKSGIVING?

KNOCK KNOCK!

WHO'S THERE?

DEWEY!

DEWEY WHO?

DEWEY WE HAVE TO KEEP WAITING
TO EAT?

KNOCK KNOCK!

WHO'S THERE?

PHIL!

PHIL WHO?

PHIL UP ANOTHER PLATE TO EAT!

KNOCK KNOCK!

WHO'S THERE?

LUKE!

LUKE WHO?

LUKE AT ALL THIS AMAZING FOOD!

KNOCK KNOCK!

WHO'S THERE?

HARRY!

HARRY WHO?

HARRY UP! IT'S TIME TO EAT.

KNOCK KNOCK!

WHO'S THERE?

DON!

DON WHO?

DON EAT ALL THE TURKEY! I WANT
SOME MORE!

KNOCK KNOCK!

WHO'S THERE?

ARTHUR!

ARTHUR WHO?

ARTHUR ANY THANKSGIVING
LEFTOVERS?

JOHNNY B. LAUGHING

ABOUT THE AUTHOR

The Joke King, Johnny B. Laughing is a best-selling joke book author. He is a jokester at heart and enjoys a good laugh, pulling pranks on his friends, and telling funny and hilarious jokes!

FOR MORE FUNNY JOKE BOOKS JUST SEARCH FOR "JOHNNY B. LAUGHING" ON AMAZON

-OR-

VISIT THE WEBSITE: WWW.FUNNY-JOKES-ONLINE.WEEBLY.COM

Made in the USA
Middletown, DE
11 November 2017